GW00393446

The du Maurier Companion

COMPILED BY STANLEY VICKERS

EDITED BY DIANA KING

FOWEY RARE BOOKS

Fowey Rare Books

4 South Street, Fowey, Cornwall. PL23 1AR. UK.
Tel: + 44 (0)1726 832 900
alexander@associates.avel.co.uk

www.cornwall-online.co.uk/envision

First Published May 1997

© **Fowey Rare Books 1997**

ISBN   1 899526 80 3

Printed by SwiftPrint, St Austell, Cornwall

Contents

Contents

ANGELA du MAURIER

GEORGE du MAURIER

FOREWORD

'First and Foremost', to quote the du Maurier family motto, I would like to thank Stanley Vickers for all the time and effort he has put into compiling this valuable register of all the literary writings of my family and forebears. Secondly, I'd like to say how much I appreciate his care and consideration in tracing the historical background of the du Maurier family and his kind words with regard to their various talents.

I feel sure that this book will be a precious asset to all du Maurier fans and indeed, a welcome introduction to the works for those still unfamiliar with the name.

The following words which conclude the prologue for her book *'Vanishing Cornwall'*, written in 1967, tells us more perhaps about Daphne du Maurier's feeling for the county, than many more famous passages found in her celebrated novels:

> *'Memories are precious things, and whether good or ill are never sad. A country known and loved in all its moods becomes woven into the pattern of life, something to be shared, to be made plain. Those born and bred in Cornwall must have the greatest understanding of its people and their ways, its history and legends, its potentiality for future growth. As one who sought to know it long ago, at five years old, in quest for freedom, and later put down roots and found content, I have come a small way on the path. The beauty and mystery beckon still'.*

Christian du Maurier Browning
Ferryside, Bodinnick
Spring 1997

INTRODUCTION

In April 1950 with my wife, Joy, we journeyed to Cornwall for the first time to spend our honeymoon in Looe. Whilst there we were taken, in an old wartime RAF air-sea rescue launch on a sea trip round to the River Fowey and up to Lerryn passing on the way the du Maurier home at Ferryside Bodinnick

Here began our discovery of the du Mauriers which has blossomed into a lifelong interest.

Our first du Maurier books came from the Companion Book Club in 1955 '*Mary Anne*', followed a year later by '*Gertrude Lawrence as Mrs A*' with its foreword by Daphne du Maurier.

With our interest awakened we collected more of Daphne's books whilst on holidays in Cornwall but the main thrust of our collection began a few years ago when my wife re-read '*Loving Spirit*' as she lay in a London Hospital recovering from surgery on her spine. From that time began an earnest search for Daphne's books both in Surrey and Cornwall. Along the way we were also to discover Angela's and George's books.

We now have an almost complete library of all the du Mauriers books together with plays, films and tapes.

In our discovery of the du Mauriers we have enjoyed together years of searching and gathering up not only the books we now possess, but also share an inexhaustible fund of memories coloured throughout by the du Maurier family.

Stanley Vickers

THE DU MAURIER STORY

The du Maurier family traces its ancestry back to the latter part of the 18th and the early years of the 19th century.

The name du Maurier comes from the La Sartha area of France to where Daphne du Maurier's great-great-grandfather Robert Mathurin Busson lived in a Chateau which his father, a master glass-blower, had rented in order to use the glassworks in the grounds, and it was Robert who extended the family sobriquet by adding the 'du Maurier', after his farmhouse birthplace, le Maurier.

The branches of the family tree came together when Ellen, the daughter of Mary Anne Clarke (nee Farquhar) married Louis-Mathurin. Mary Anne had been the mistress of George III's second son Frederick, the Duke of York 1763-1827 and a whiff of corruption followed her when it was alleged that he permitted Mrs Clarke too much influence in the granting of commissions to her financial gain. He was removed from the head of the Army but reinstated in 1811.

Ellen and Louis-Mathurin had three children, the eldest born in Paris in March 1834 was named George Louis Palmella Busson du Maurier. It was in George that the exceptional artistic and literary talent which permeates all generations of du Mauriers to this day, was first revealed.

George du Maurier studied art in Paris and his Anglo-French background was to characterise his personality, his art and his writings for the whole of his life. Whilst living in Antwerp, George lost the sight of his left eye and, worried about his sight, he travelled to Dusseldorf to consult a world famous oculist. In Dusseldorf he met up with the Wightwicks, a family he had previously known in London. Finding himself falling in love with their daughter Emma, he travelled back to London with them and eventually married her in 1863.

George du Maurier's immense talent and artistic skill led eventually to his appointment to the staff of Punch where for more than thirty years, from 1865, he produced two sharp and beautifully drawn cartoons a week. He and his wife with their children settled in Hampstead where during the last years of his life, he wrote three novels, the last in the year of his death 1897. Two of his other books were published posthumously in 1898.

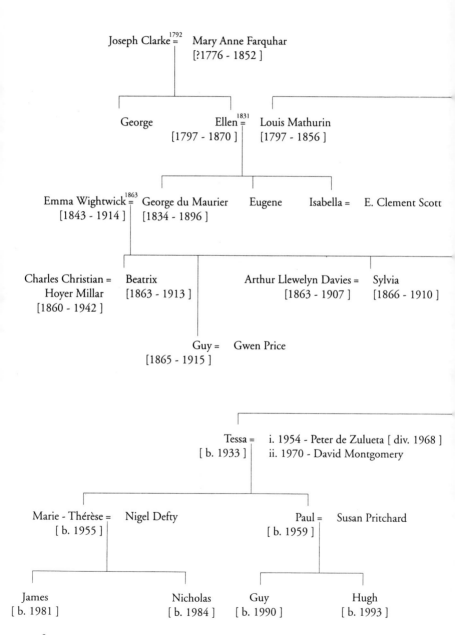

Joseph Clarke =[1792] Mary Anne Farquhar
[?1776 - 1852]

George   Ellen =[1831] Louis Mathurin
[1797 - 1870]   [1797 - 1856]

Emma Wightwick =[1863] George du Maurier   Eugene   Isabella =   E. Clement Scott
[1843 - 1914]   [1834 - 1896]

Charles Christian =   Beatrix   Arthur Llewelyn Davies =   Sylvia
Hoyer Millar   [1863 - 1913]   [1863 - 1907]   [1866 - 1910]
[1860 - 1942]

Guy =   Gwen Price
[1865 - 1915]

Tessa =   i. 1954 - Peter de Zulueta [div. 1968]
[b. 1933]   ii. 1970 - David Montgomery

Marie - Thérèse =   Nigel Defty   Paul =   Susan Pritchard
[b. 1955]   [b. 1959]

James   Nicholas   Guy   Hugh
[b. 1981]   [b. 1984]   [b. 1990]   [b. 1993]

THE DU MAURIER FAMILY TREE

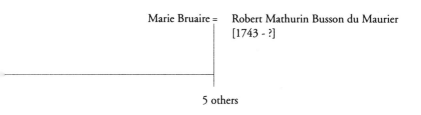

Marie Bruaire = Robert Mathurin Busson du Maurier
[1743 - ?]

5 others

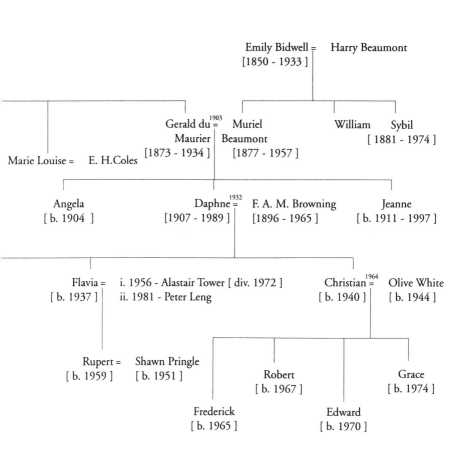

Emily Bidwell = Harry Beaumont
[1850 - 1933]

Gerald du =¹⁹⁰³ Muriel   William   Sybil
Maurier   Beaumont   [1881 - 1974]
[1873 - 1934] [1877 - 1957]

Marie Louise = E. H. Coles

Angela   Daphne =¹⁹³² F. A. M. Browning   Jeanne
[b. 1904]   [1907 - 1989] [1896 - 1965]   [b. 1911 - 1997]

Flavia = i. 1956 - Alastair Tower [div. 1972]   Christian =¹⁹⁶⁴ Olive White
[b. 1937] ii. 1981 - Peter Leng   [b. 1940] [b. 1944]

Rupert = Shawn Pringle   Robert   Grace
[b. 1959] [b. 1951]   [b. 1967]   [b. 1974]

Frederick   Edward
[b. 1965]   [b. 1970]

9

The youngest child of Emma and George du Maurier was Daphne's father Gerald born in 1873. He became an acclaimed actor and producer who later in life was knighted for his services to the theatre and charity. Gerald's first stage success was in 1902 at the Duke of York's Theatre playing opposite Muriel Beaumont in J.M. Barrie's 'The Admirable Crichton'. This stage meeting led to romance and marriage and the birth of three daughters, Angela in 1904, Daphne in 1907 and Jeanne in 1911.

Encouraged by their father, the girls all showed a flair for play acting and often entertained their parents' guests. All three girls in time were to develop an interest in art or writing linking them it would seem to their grandfather George du Maurier. It was Daphne du Maurier who as a teenager began writing short stories.

In 1926 Muriel and her three daughters travelled to Cornwall with the intention of purchasing a holiday home. They spent the night in Looe then drove the few miles to the hamlet of Bodinnick on the opposite shore of the river to Fowey.

They spotted a 'For Sale' notice on a dilapidated boat-house known locally as Swiss Cottage. Their search which had hardly begun was over, the boat-house soon purchased and renamed 'Ferryside'. It has remained in the du Maurier family ever since.

The purchase of Ferryside changed Daphne's life for ever and a year later, on her twentieth birthday, 13th May 1927, she was allowed to stay behind on her own when her mother and Angela returned to London. Day after day she explored the countryside on both sides of the River Fowey combining the writing of short stories with her outings.

On one of her walks she came upon the rotting hulk of an old schooner stuck in the mud of Pont Pill. Still visible was the old figurehead bearing the name, Jane Slade. Unknowingly, Daphne had stumbled on the subject of her first full length novel. When researching the origin of the schooner, she discovered it had been built in the local boatyard owned by the Slades, and Jane Slade was buried in the nearby Lanteglos churchyard. In the novel Jane Slade becomes 'Janet Coombe' and the local town of Polruan is 'Plyn'. In describing the wedding of Janet Coombe in '*The Loving Spirit*', Daphne foretells her own marriage to Major (Boy) Browning in St Wyllow Church on 19th July 1932. Some years after publication of this novel, the figurehead was removed from the wreck and presented to Daphne who had it mounted on a beam below her bedroom window, where it remains to this day.

In the fifty years following the publication of her first novel, Daphne du Maurier wrote a further sixteen novels and nine other books including her biographies and over fifty short stories, as well as numerous articles in other books, but it is for those stories set in Cornwall that she is now world famous. Her books have been translated into every major language.

Daphne lived for most of her adult life around the Fowey area, first at Menabilly and latterly at Kilmarth where on 19th April 1989, a few weeks before her eighty-second birthday, she died.

Angela du Maurier (born 1904) began writing just prior to the Second World War. She wrote nine novels in all, a volume of short stories and three volumes of autobiographical reminiscences. For many years she lived at Ferryside, and now in her nineties she lives in London.

Jeanne du Maurier (born 1911), the youngest of the three sisters, lived on Dartmoor. She became a well known artist and had several exhibitions. Her paintings have been hung in the Royal Academy Summer Exhibition on several occasions. She was also a gifted pianist, a hobby she enjoyed up until her death in January 1997.

In the next generation, **Lady Flavia Leng**, Daphne's second daughter, followed in the steps of her great-grandfather George du Maurier and studied art in Paris. She designed book covers for her mother and in 1994 published her own book, *Daphne du Maurier - a Daughter's Memoir*. In it Flavia describes her childhood in London and in Cornwall at Menabilly. She reveals her mother as a writer deeply attached to Cornwall where she has found inspiration for her novels. She portrays her as living a quiet and private life of her own choosing, only reluctantly becoming involved in social occasions.

Christian du Maurier Browning, Daphne's son, now lives at Ferryside and runs du Maurier Productions Ltd., the company responsible for films, theatre, television and radio productions of his mother's work.

No appreciation of the du Mauriers could conclude without an expression of the debt of gratitude owed to them for the pleasures, both artistic and literary, they have presented to the world.

Synopsis of Daphne du Maurier Books And Plays.

The Loving Spirit

~ published on 23rd February 1931 by Heineman in London and in New York by Doubleday

Daphne's first novel, written when she was just 23 years old and living at Ferryside, Bodinnick, is essentially the story of a woman's enduring love which passes down through three generations of her family. Based on the lives of a ship-building family in the area, the matriarch of the family ~ Janet Coombe ~ is born with a passion for the sea and the great ships which sail upon it. Her 'loving spirit' is passed on to her beloved son Joseph and reappears finally in her great-granddaughter Jennifer, with whom the saga ends.

The concept of 'time lapse' which makes this story so compelling, is one which Daphne returns to in many of her subsequent novels, and one which obviously fascinated her from an early age.

I'll Never Be Young Again

~ published in May 1932 by Heineman. London and in New York by Doubleday.

Daphne's second novel was written in London in an office loaned to her by her godmother, in Orange St, Leicester Square. It was completed on 18th July 1930, taking only two months to write.

In this novel a young man is about to throw himself off Waterloo Bridge. A passer-by prevents him from taking his own life and together they embark on a series of adventures. The young man's path eventually leads him to Paris where he sets up home with a teacher of music, but ultimately returns home to become a respectable citizen.

JULIUS

~ published in the spring of 1933 by Heineman. London and in New York by Doubleday. Previously published as *The Progress of Julius.*

Daphne's third novel. The plot for this novel formed in her mind whilst in Paris in January 1931 and was completed at Ferryside later the same year. Beginning against the background of the Franco -Prussian war, the story continues until the 1930's. It is a grim and disturbing tale of an obsessive man's progress from extreme poverty to unimaginable wealth and ultimately a lonely, embittered old age. His overpowering love for his only daughter ~ in part reciprocated ~ leads to a dramatic and terrible conclusion.

GERALD - A PORTRAIT

~ published in November 1934, by Victor Gollancz Ltd. London and in 1935 by Doubleday of New York.

Gerald died aged sixty one on 11th. April 1934. Within six months of his death Daphne had published his biography. At the time, the book was considered to be deeply shocking in that she wrote extremely candidly about her father. To his admiring public for whom he had been an idol without flaw, the revelation of his many love affairs (albeit before his marriage) proved distressing. However, reviewers gave the book a favourable though muted approval.

JAMAICA INN

~ First published January 1936 by Victor Gollancz Ltd London and in New York by Doubleday.

Daphne's fourth novel. In October 1935 Daphne wrote a note for the fore leaf of this novel, it says

> 'Jamaica Inn stands today, hospitable and kindly, a temperance house on the twenty-mile road between Bodmin and Launceston. In the following story I have pictured it as it might have been over 120 years ago. A tale of smuggling and other evil doings around Jamaica Inn and Bodmin Moor'.

THE DU MAURIERS

~ First published January 1937 by Victor Gollancz Ltd London and in New York by Doubleday.

A biography of the du Maurier family from 1810. A dedication in the front of this book was to the 31 descendants of Louis-Mathurin Busson du Maurier alive in October 1936. Daphne then age 29, was the great-great-grand-daughter of Mathurin-Robert Busson du Maurier on one side and Mary Anne Clarke (Mistress of the Duke of York) on the other side.

REBECCA

~ Published by Victor Gollancz Ltd. in 1938, and in New York by Doubleday.

Daphne's fifth novel begins with the now famous words 'Last night I dreamt I went to Manderley again' The story which unfolds is known to millions of readers, and has been performed on stage, film and TV. The idea for the novel began to grow in the author's mind when she was staying in Alexandria in Egypt in 1937. The opening words are spoken by the narrator, a young unsophisticated girl whose love for the wealthy widower Max de Winter is haunted by the mysterious death of his first wife, Rebecca of the title. The brooding tale is overshadowed throughout by the hostile presence of Mrs Danvers, the housekeeper of Manderley, the Cornish country mansion modelled in part on Menabilly.

COME WIND COME WEATHER

~ Published by Heineman in 1940 and in 1941 by Doubleday in New York.

A collection of wartime stories compiled by Daphne du Maurier for the Oxford Group Moral Re-Armament Movement. First published in August it contained the following short stories:

Come Wind, Come Weather	Physician Heal Thyself
The Admiralty Regrets	Spitfire Megan
George and Jimmy	The Revolutionary
Over the Ration Books	London 1940?
A Nation's Strength	Miss Hill and the Soldiers
A Miner's Tale	

The book concludes with an Epilogue. A new and revised edition was published in November 1940, in this version *The Revolutionary* was omitted and a new story *In a London Air-Raid Shelter* was added. The Epilogue was re-written and extended. Both editions sold for sixpence with royalties from the sales going to the charity 'The Soldiers', Sailors' and Airmen's Association.

FRENCHMAN'S CREEK

~ Published by Victor Gollancz Ltd in 1941 and in 1942 by Doubleday New York.

Daphne's sixth novel. The story begins with the words 'When the east wind blows up Helford river....'. Daphne returns to the river on which she spent her honeymoon for the location of the story. The beautiful Lady Dona finds excitement and passion in the arms of a French pirate who anchors his ship in secret in 'Frenchman's Creek'.

HUNGRY HILL

~ Published by Victor Gollancz Ltd. in London 1943 and by Doubleday New York.

Daphne's seventh novel. A passionate story of five generations of an Irish family and of the copper mine with which their fortunes and fate were closely linked.

THE YEARS BETWEEN

~ A play published in 1945 by Samuel French Ltd. Published in book form by Victor Gollancz Ltd. in the following year 1946.

First produced on the stage at the Opera House, Manchester on 20th November 1944. All the action takes place in the library of a country house. Col. Wentworth, a Conservative MP, is reported lost at sea in an aircraft crash during the early part of the Second World War. In his absence Mrs Wentworth is appointed an MP in his place, falls in love with a close friend and plans to marry him. However, before this can take place, the Colonel reappears shortly before the War ends.

THE KINGS GENERAL

~ Published by Victor Gollancz Ltd in 1946, and in New York by Doubleday.

Daphne's eighth novel and her first to be written while living at Menabilly. The story is closely linked with the fortunes of the Rashleigh family, owners of Menabilly, and is recounted against the background of the Civil War and its effects in Cornwall.

SEPTEMBER TIDE

~ A play. 1949 Victor Gollancz Ltd London and in 1960 by Doubleday New York.

First produced on stage in the New Theatre, Oxford in November 1948 transferring to the Aldwych in December of the same year. The leading part was taken by Gertrude Lawrence. The story suggests a love affair between a mother and her daughter's husband, the action taking place in the mother's home on a river estuary. The play will once again be performed during the Daphne du Maurier Festival taking place in and around Fowey during May 1997 to celebrate her life and work in Cornwall.

THE PARASITES

~ Published by Victor Gollancz Ltd. London during 1949 and in 1950 in New York by Doubleday.

Daphne's ninth novel. A richly gifted and bohemian family, in many ways the Delaneys mirror the talents of the du Mauriers themselves, but here any similarity ends! The Delaneys, arrogant, egotistical and self-serving, represent the parasites of the title, each living in some way off one another.

This book was completed at Menabilly in the spring of 1949.

THE YOUNG GEORGE DU MAURIER

~ Edited and published by Peter Davies 1951

A volume of letters 1860-70 with some of George's sketches edited by Daphne du Maurier.

MY COUSIN RACHEL

~ Published by Victor Gollancz Ltd. in London in 1951, and in 1952 in New York by Doubleday.

Daphne's tenth novel. This is the story of two cousins, Ambrose and Philip, and their consuming passion for the beautiful but enigmatic Rachel of the title. When one of the cousins marries her and then dies in mysterious circumstances, the other sets out to discover for himself what really happened. He too falls under the spell of the charming Rachel, and is finally left, like the reader, with the unanswered question as to her involvement in his cousin's death. This story was set in the Cornwall and Italy of the last century.

MARY ANNE

~ Published by Victor Gollancz Ltd in London 1954, and in New York by Doubleday.

Daphne's eleventh novel was based on the history of her ancestor in the Regency period, Mary Anne Clarke. It is the story of a beautiful Cockney girl who finds herself in the familiar situation of struggling to raise four children with nothing but a drunken husband and a wastrel brother for support. She decides to exploit the only asset she possesses ~ herself ~ and in doing so finally becomes the mistress of the Duke of York. However, not content with this, she begins to sell military information acquired in the privacy of the bed chamber. Eventually the scandal rocks the entire country, resulting in the Duke of York becoming involved in Court proceedings.

THE SCAPEGOAT

~ Published by Victor Gollancz Ltd London in 1957, and in New York by Doubleday.

Daphne's twelfth novel. An Englishman in France unexpectedly meets his double, a French Count, and through an intriguing device becomes the scapegoat for the sins of the charming and idle French aristocrat.

For just one week their lives are transposed, but it is when the Englishman decides to return to his true persona that the macabre twist to the tale is revealed.

THE INFERNAL WORLD OF BRANWELL BRONTE

~ Published by Victor Gollancz Ltd. 1960 and in New York in 1961 by Doubleday.

A biography of Patrick Branwell Bronte, brother of the Bronte sisters The story of a drunken reprobate dying at thirty-one from the result of his own excesses. Modern eyes may judge him more gently than once his own family did.

We can recognise the epilepsy the retreat behind laudanum or alcohol, the first shadows of schizophrenia, and we can understand the sense of failure in the precocious young man who could not get one couplet published and whose erratic behaviour prevented the holding of the humblest job.

Excluded out of misguided kindness from his sisters' success and in the face of the world's censure and his own shame, he returns to his scribbled world of childhood wickedness - the infernal world where he truly belonged.

CASTLE DOR

~ With Sir Arthur Quiller-Couch, published by J.M. Dent and Sons Ltd in 1962, and by Doubleday in New York.

This is the re-telling, against the background of nineteenth century Cornwall and its people of one of the saddest love stories of all time, the story of Tristan and Iseult.

The novel was begun by Sir Arthur Quiller-Couch. After his death his daughter Foy, a friend of Daphne du Maurier asked her to complete the book. The result is a spellbinding love story closely linked to Castle Dor and Fowey.

Daphne du Maurier at Menabilly near Fowey. c.1946.

Ferryside, set into the cliff face on the banks of the River Fowey, was originally a boat-builder's yard. Purchased by the du Maurier family in 1926, it was the place where Daphne wrote her first novel, *The Loving Spirit*, and met her future husband.

Photograph by Rob Jacksay.

Shown below are a selection of covers from various Daphne du Maurier titles.

Shown above are a selection of more covers from various Daphne du Maurier titles.

THE GLASS BLOWERS

~ First published by Victor Gollancz Ltd. In 1963, and in New York by Doubleday.

Daphne's fourteenth novel is a semi-biographical novel based upon the story of her forefathers before and during the French Revolution. The Bussons were a family of master glass-blowers and took the du Maurier name from a farm. The Louis XV engraved crystal tumbler made by the Bussons and handed down through the family was in Daphne's possession at the time this novel was written

THE FLIGHT OF THE FALCON

~ Published by Victor Gollancz Ltd. London in 1965.

Daphne's fifteenth novel. Although truly fictional, the story was inspired by an existing Italian university. Over five hundred years ago, Duke Claudio, 'The Falcon', lived his brutal twisted life in the city of Ruffano. Five centuries later the town had forgotten its violent history.

Within the new University a Professor seeks to bring back to life the final flight of the Falcon and through murder, humiliation and outrage almost succeeds. A gripping and suspense-laden novel written whilst Daphne was still living at Menabilly.

VANISHING CORNWALL

~ Published by Victor Gollancz Ltd London in 1967.

Daphne writes about the Cornwall she loves and which has given her the ideas for many of her novels. Together with her son Christian she sets out to record what she knows of the old Cornwall which she believes is vanishing under the invasion of tourism. Her son took the photographs in the ensuing book, which was later re-issued in 1981 in full colour.

THE HOUSE ON THE STRAND

~ Published in 1969 by Victor Gollancz Ltd.

The idea for this, her sixteenth novel, came to Daphne when she found preserved embryos and other intriguing yet macabre items left behind in the cellar of Kilmarth, the house into which she was moving after twenty six years in Menabilly. The novel links Kilmarth with fourteenth century Tywardreath, a nearby village, in time warp sequences involving the present day narrator in the lives of a long-dead family, with tragic consequences.

RULE BRITANNIA

~ Daphne's seventeenth and final novel. Published by Victor Gollancz Ltd London in 1972 and in New York Doubleday 1973.

Written when Daphne was sixty two years old and living at Kilmarth, the story is of Britain leaving the European confederation and joining the United States in a new alliance. Far from being an alliance, America assumes the dominant role and attempts to subdue the country. The Cornish population rebels, and the American Marines land in Par Bay.

This novel is totally different from any of Daphne's previous work.

GOLDEN LADS

~ Published by Victor Gollancz Ltd London in 1975, and in New York by Doubleday 1975.

A study of Anthony Bacon, Francis Bacon and their friends.

Following the publication of her last novel, *Rule Britannia*, and now settled in Kilmarth, Daphne turned her mind to a historical subject.

After extensive research of records and letters both in France and England the 'Golden Lads' tells the story of Anthony and Francis Bacon linked to Queen Elizabeth 1 through their friendship with the Earl of Essex. Anthony acted as agent in France collecting intelligence information for the Earl. Francis was compelled by the Queen to charge the Earl of Essex with treason for which the Earl was beheaded on the 25th February 1601. Anthony died on the 21st May 1601. Francis lived on to become Lord Chancellor and Lord Keeper. He went on to win fame as a writer and philosopher.

THE WINDING STAIRS

~ Published in 1976 by Victor Gollancz Ltd and by Doubleday New York. in 1977.

The Life and Times of Francis Bacon.

When Anthony died in 1601 his brother Francis was forty years of age, he was to live for another twenty-five years, becoming successively Solicitor-General, Attorney-General, a member of the Privy Council and Lord Chancellor. He became Baron Venilum and finally Viscount St. Alban. His literary works were extensive and added to philosophical and scientific writings embraced the extraordinary complexity of Francis Bacon's character.

He married a girl much younger than himself but they never had any family. Francis aged sixty was impeached by both Houses of Parliament on charges of Bribery and Corruption He pleaded guilty and was sentenced, fined £40,000 and imprisoned in the Tower. He never again held office or sat in Parliament.

GROWING PAINS

~ *The Shaping of a Writer*. Published by Victor Gollancz Ltd in 1977.(Published since 1979 as '*Myself When Young ~ The Shaping of a Writer*' same publisher).

In this autobiography Daphne writes of her early life from the time she was a very small child until the age of twenty five when her first novel (*The Loving Spirit*) had been published and she had met and married her husband.

Much of what she has written was contained in her personal diaries which she kept from 1920 when she was twelve years old until 1932 when she married.

THE REBECCA NOTEBOOK AND OTHER MEMORIES

~ Published by Victor Gollancz Ltd London in 1981.

The book is full of Daphne's memories and follows on from her autobiography, *Myself when Young.*. She tells how *Rebecca* was conceived and written.

She gives her views on romantic love, religion, success, death and widowhood, and writes of her life in the various homes which became so dear to her.

Here is a collection that shows something of Daphne's great talent and reveals her as a person of immense strength of character, a wide range of interests and a delightful sense of humour.

It gives much insight into her mastery of the writers craft and a glimpse of the inner vision which has made her novels so memorable.

OMNIBUS EDITIONS

The Daphne du Maurier Omnibus

Published 1956 (including *Rebecca, Jamaica Inn* and *Frenchman's Creek)*

The Daphne du Maurier Tandem

Published 1964 (including *Mary Anne* and *My Cousin Rachel)*

Three Famous du Maurier Novels

Published 1982 (*The Flight of the Falcon, The House on the Strand* and *The Kings' General)*

Four Great Cornish Novels

Published 1982 (including *Jamaica Inn, Rebecca, Frenchman's Creek* and *My Cousin Rachel)*

All these Omnibus Edition published by Victor Gollancz Ltd.

SHORT STORIES

Happy Christmas

~ Published by Todd London 1943.
New York Doubleday 1940.

Consider The Lilies

~Published by Todd, London 1943 p.b.

Escort

~Published by Todd London 1943 p.b.

Nothing Hurts For Long

~Published by Todd 1943 p.b.

Spring Picture

~Published by Todd 1944 p.b. ~ later
published as *The Closing Door.*

Leading Lady

~Published by Vallancey Press
London 1945 p.b.

London And Paris

~Published by Vallancey Press London
1945 p.b.

The Apple Tree

~Published by Victor Gollancz Ltd
London 1952 and in New York by
Doubleday 1953. Published since 1963
as *The Birds and Other Stories.*

Early Stories

~ Published by Todd, London 1955.

The Breaking Point

~Published by Victor Gollancz Ltd
London 1959. Published since 1970 as
The Blue Lenses.

The Treasury of du Maurier Short Stories

~including all the stories in *The Apple
Tree and The Breaking Point* —
Published in 1960.

The Lover

~ Published in 1961.

Not After Midnight

~ Published by Victor Gollancz Ltd. in
1971. Published since 1973 as
Don't Look Now .

Echoes From The Macabre

~ Published in 1976 by Victor Gollancz
Ltd and Doubleday New York 1977.

The Rendezvous And Other Stories

~ Published by Victor Gollancz Ltd
in 1980.

Classics Of The Macabre

~ Published by Victor Gollancz Ltd
London in 1987.

List of all Daphne du Maurier short stories and the volumes in which they are published

Story	Happy Christmas	Consider the Lilies	Escort	Nothing Hurts for Long & Escort	Spring Picture	Leading Lady	London And Paris	The Apple Tree/The Birds & Other Stories	Early Stories (Todd)	The Breaking Point / The Blue Lenses	The Treasury of Short Stories	The Lover	Not After Midnight / Don't Look Now	Echoes From the Macabre	The Rendezvous & Other Stories	Classics of the Macabre
Adieu Sagesse									●						●	
The Alibi										●	●					●
Angels and Archangels									●						●	
The Apple Tree								●			●			●		●
The Archduchess										●	●					
The Birds								●			●			●		●
The Blue Lenses										●	●			●		●
A Borderline Case													●			
The Breakthrough													●			
The Chamois										●	●			●		
The Closing Door									●						●	
Consider the Lilies		●														
A Difference in Temperament									●							
Don't Look Now													●	●		●
Escort			●	●											●	
Fairy Tale									●						●	
Frustration									●							
Ganymede										●	●					
And now to God the Father									●							
Happy Christmas	●															
Indiscretion									●						●	
Kiss me again Stranger								●			●			●		
La Sainte-Vierge									●						●	
Leading Lady						●			●						●	
The Little Photographer								●			●					
London and Paris							●									
The Lordly Ones										●	●					
The Lover									●			●			●	
Mazie									●							
The Menace										●	●					
Monte Verita								●			●					
No Motive															●	
Not After Midnight													●	●		●
Nothing Hurts for Long				●					●							
The Old Man								●			●			●		
Panic									●						●	
Picadilly									●							
The Pool										●	●			●		
The Rendezvous															●	
Split Second															●	
Spring Picture					●											
The Supreme Artist									●						●	
Tame Cat									●							
The Way of the Cross													●			
Weekend									●							

PLAYS

1939 **Rebecca**

~ Gollancz, An adaptation by Daphne du Maurier of her own novel ~ Samuel French Ltd in playform.

1945 **The Years Between**

~ Gollancz, A play written by Daphne du Maurier ~ Samuel French Ltd in playform.

1949 **September Tide**

~ A play written by Daphne du Maurier ~ Gollancz and New York 1960.

1976 **The Breakthrough**

~ A short story made into a television drama for the BBC.

1979 **My Cousin Rachel**

~ A play by Diana Morgan based on the novel ~ Samuel French Ltd. in playform and du Maurier Productions Ltd.

1979 **The Little Photographer**

~ A play by Derek Hoddinott and du Maurier Productions Ltd based on a short story ~ Samuel French Ltd in playform.

1994 **Rebecca**

~ A play by Clifford Williams and du Maurier Productions Ltd based on the novel. Samuel French Ltd in playform.

FILMS MADE FROM DAPHNE DU MAURIER TITLES

Jamaica Inn

~ Made in 1939 by Mayflower and
directed by Alfred Hitchcock.

Rebecca

~ Made in 1940 by David O Selznick
and direct by Alfred Hitchcock.

Frenchman's Creek

~ Made in 1943 by Paramount and
directed by Mitchell Leison

Hungry Hill

~ Made in 1945 by G.F.D/Two Cities
and directed by Brian Desmond Hurst.

The Years Between

~ Made in 1947 by G.F.D/Sydney Box
and directed by Compton Bennett.

My Cousin Rachel

~ Made in 1953 by Twentieth Century
Fox and directed by Henry Koster.

The Scapegoat

~ Made in 1959 by M.G.M. and
directed by Robert Hamer.

The Birds

~ Made in 1963 by Universal Studios and directed by Alfred Hitchcock.

Don't Look Now

~ Made in 1973 by British Lion and directed by Nick Roeg.

The Breakthrough

~ Made for Television in 1993 by World International Network Television Distribution and directed by Piers Haggard.

Rebecca

~ Made for Television in 1996. A Portman Production for Carlton TV.

VIDEO TAPES

1971 Vanishing Cornwall
> ~ Directed by Christian Browning.

1977 The Make Believe World Of Daphne du Maurier
> ~ A film by Christian Browning to celebrate the seventieth birthday of Daphne du Maurier and the publication of her autobiography *'Myself When Young'* ~ made for the ITV network with Cliff Michelmore.

1990 My Cousin Rachel
> ~ Dramatised by Hugh Whitemore for BBC Enterprises.

1993 Rebecca
> ~ A video of the original 1940 B/W film. Directed by Alfred Hitchcock.

1997 Rebecca
> ~ Video of the 1997 Production by Carlton Television.

AUDIO ~ CASSETTES (AUDIOBOOKS)

A popular range of Daphne du Maurier's novels are available on audio, both full length and abridged versions.

LIST OF BOOKS WITH A FOREWORD, STORY OR AN ARTICLE WRITTEN BY DAPHNE DU MAURIER

Also books written about her or other members of the du Maurier family.

1931 The Best Stories of 1931

⁓ Edited by Edward J O'Brien, includes *Panic* by Daphne du Maurier.

1939 The Queen's Book of the Red Cross

⁓With a message from Her Majesty the Queen and contributions by fifty British authors and artists. Daphne du Maurier contributes her short story *The Escort*.

1946 Countryside Character

⁓ compiled by Richard Harman ⁓ A collection of articles about the British countryside written by many famous authors. Daphne du Maurier contributes *The House Of Secrets*.

1954 Gertrude Lawrence as 'Mrs A'

⁓ an intimate biography of the great star by her husband Richard Stoddard Aldrich. Published again in 1956 by the Companion Book Club when Daphne wrote the foreword. Daphne appears in one of the photographs, meeting 'Mrs A' on her arrival in London.

1963 **Best Stories of Phyllis Bottome**
- Twenty five stories chosen, with a preface by Daphne du Maurier.

1965 After the death of her husband, Major-General Sir Frederick (Boy) Browning, Daphne du Maurier wrote an article for CRUSE, (bereavement care charity). This is available as a leaflet entitled *Death And Widowhood*. This article also appears in **The Rebecca Notebook and other Memories.**

1966 **What I Believe**
- edited by George Unwin. A collection of nineteen personal philosophies including one by Daphne du Maurier.

1969 **George du Maurier**
- a biography by Leonée Ormond. Published by Routledge Keegan Paul.

1970 **By Royal Appointment** by Paul Berry.
- A biography of Mary Ann Clarke Daphne du Maurier's great-great-grandmother (Mistress of the Duke of York).

1972 **Letters from a Cornish Garden** (Trelowarren) by Lady C C Vyvyan.
- Daphne du Maurier wrote the foreword to this book. Published by Michael Joseph.

1973 My Cornwall

~ a collection of articles written by eleven well known authors edited by Michael Williams. In this book Daphne du Maurier contributed *The Claw Of Cornwall* and Angela du Maurier wrote *Fowey.* Published by Bossiney Books.

1974 Cornish Harvest

~ edited by Denys Val Baker. An anthology of short stories written by sixteen well known authors. Daphne du Maurier contributed *The Pool.*

1979 King Arthur Country in Cornwall

~ Bossiney Books. There are references to Daphne du Maurier mainly in connection with *Castle Dor* and *Vanishing Cornwall.*

1987 Victor Gollancz

~ a biography by Ruth Dudley Edwards. Contains many references to Daphne du Maurier and her dealings with Victor Gollancz.

1987 Daphne du Maurier Country

~ by Martyn Shallcross.

1989 Friends and Contemporaries

~ by A L Rowse. This book contains the record of his friendship with Daphne du Maurier in the chapter headed *Daphne du Maurier ~ Fortune and Romance.*

1989 **Daphne du Maurier - Enchanted Cornwall - Her Pictorial Memoir**
~ edited by Piers Dudgeon.

1989 **Gerald du Maurier**
~ a biography by James Harding.

1991 **Forever England**
~ an evaluation of Femininity, Literature and Conservatism between the Wars by Alison Light. Chapter IV ~ Daphne du Maurier's romance with the past.

1991 **Daphne**
~ a portrait of Daphne du Maurier by Judith Cook. Bantam Press.

1991 **The Private World of Daphne du Maurier**
~ by Martyn Shallcross. Robson Books.

1992 **Daphne du Maurier - Letters from Menabilly - Portrait of a Friendship**
~ edited by Oriel Malet. Published by M Evans.

1993 **A Biography of Daphne du Maurier**
~ by Margaret Forster. Published by Chatto Windus.

1993 **Mrs de Winter**
~ The sequel to Daphne du Maurier's *Rebecca* by Susan Hill.

1994 Daphne du Maurier - A Daughter's Memoir
~ by Lady Flavia Leng. Mainstream Publishing.

1995 The Cornish World of Daphne du Maurier
~ Published by Bossiney Books ~ includes *Eccentrics* a previously un-published work by Daphne du Maurier.

1995 Daphne du Maurier's Cornwall - Her Pictorial Memoir
~ edited by Piers Dudgeon. An abridged version of *Enchanted Cornwall* (previously published in 1989). The majority of the photographs are new to this book and are by Christian Browning.

1996 Cornwall
~ by Philip Payton, published by Alexander Associates. Pages 261- 262 contain references to Daphne du Maurier's novels, which the author states identified her overwhelmingly with Cornwall.

ANGELA DU MAURIER

NOVELS

The Perplexed Heart	~ Published by Peter Davies, 1939.
The Spinning Wheel	~ Published by Peter Davies, 1940.
The Little Less	~ Published by Peter Davies, 1941.
Treveryan	~ Published by Peter Davies, 1942.
Lawrence Vane	~ Published by Peter Davies, 1946.
Reveille	~ Published by Peter Davies, 1950.
Shallow Waters	~ Published by Peter Davies, 1952.
The Road To Leenane	~ Published by Peter Davies, 1963.
The Frailty Of Nature	~ Published by Peter Davies, 1969.

SHORT STORIES

Birkinshaw And Other Stories
~ Published by Peter Davies, 1948 A collection of twelve short stories.

AUTOBIOGRAPHIES

Its Only The Sister　　~ Published by Peter Davies, 1951.

Old Maids Remember

~ Published by Peter Davies, 1966. A book of memoirs arranged in alphabetical sequence of subjects.

Pilgrims By The Way　　~ Published by Peter Davies, 1967.

GEORGE DU MAURIER 1834 - 1896
PUBLISHED WORKS.

RECOLLECTIONS OF AN ENGLISH GOLDMINE

~ Once A Week V. (21 September 1861) pp.356-364, 186.

ENGLISH SOCIETY AT HOME:

From The Collection Of Mr Punch ~ Published by Bradbury Agnew and Co. 1880.

THE ILLUSTRATION OF BOOKS FROM THE SERIOUS ARTIST'S POINT OF VIEW

~ *Magazine of Art.* pp.349-353 and 371-375, August and September 1890.

PETER IBBETSON

~First published in Harper's Monthly Magazine XXII, June to November 1891.

Begun in 1889 when George du Maurier was 55 years old, this novel surprised those who knew his previous works for the romantic intensity of its theme. In essence he is recounting the happiness of his own childhood and the poignancy of growing up and entering the 'real world'.

The hero leaves his beloved French home to live in England under the guardianship of an uncle whom he hates. Becoming increasingly unhappy, and separated irreconcilably from his childhood sweetheart, he escapes from reality by teaching himself to 'dream true'. In this trance-like state he can return to his old home where he continues the life he would like to have led with the beautiful Mimsey, now a Duchess in the real world.

Events all too real take a violent and eventually tragic turn for Peter, but throughout he can escape to his dream-world, where at the end of his life he does in fact find solace.

TRILBY

~ First published in Harper's Monthly Magazine XXVII-XXVIII (January to July 1887), 1894.

This classic romantic thriller is richly evocative of the student days du Maurier spent in Paris and is the story of Trilby O'Ferrall, an artist's model. A resounding success, it first appeared in three volumes. Trilby was dramatised by Paul Potter and played to packed houses at Her Majesty's Theatre in London. So popular was the book and the play that toothpaste, collars, soap, songs, a dance and even a town in America were named after the heroine. However the name has lasted longest of all with the soft felt hat that Trilby wore on stage.

THE MARTIAN

~ First published in Harper's Monthly Magazine, XXXII-XXXIV (October 1896 to July 1897) Published posthumously, 1897

Although ostensibly a novel, with The Martian being the spirit of a woman who controlled the life of the hero, Barty Josselin, the book is a thinly disguised autobiography of George du Maurier, or perhaps the life he would have liked to have led.

SOCIAL PICTORIAL SATIRE

~ A satirical description of the art of sketching with illustrations. Published by Harper and Collins, London and New York, 1898. First published in Harper's Monthly Magazine XXXVI (February to March 1898).

A LEGEND OF CAMELOT

~ Pictures and Poems, 1898.

OMNIBUS EDITION ~ PETER IBBETSON, TRILBY AND THE MARTIAN.

Published by Peter Davies, with an introduction by John Masefield and Daphne du Maurier, 1947.

In a 1969 edition of **Peter Ibbetson** the preface was also written by Daphne du Maurier.

Books and articles directly
Concerned with George du Maurier

1897 'George du Maurier in Hampstead,'
~ *Hampstead Annual*, pp;12-19.

1912 'Reminiscences of George du Maurier'
~ in Thomas Armstrong C.B.
A Memoir, edited by L.M.Lamont.

1895 'Mr du Maurier at Home'
~ *Idler*, VIII 9 (December 1895)
pp: 415-422.

1895 Trilbyana: The Rise and Progress of a Popular Novel
~New York 1895.

1883 'George du Maurier and London Society'
~ *Century Magazine*, XXXVI pp:48-65.

1940 'Un Anglo-Francais Georges du Maurier'
~ *Revue de Paris* pp:236-281

1896 In Bohemia with du Maurier
~ by F. Moscheles.

1913 George du Maurier - The Satirist of the Victorians;
~ A Review of His Art and his
Personality.